A MUSICAL FRACTURED FAIRYTALE

Book and lyrics by
S. J. Henschel

Music and additional lyrics by
Jim Schmitt

GOTTA DANCE!

For all stage performance inquiries, please contact:

Steele Spring Stage Rights
3845 Cazador Street
Los Angeles, CA 90065
(323) 739-0413

www.stagerights.com

CHARACTERS

KING VARIBALD – Male, 30s to 50s. The king of the enchanted land.

QUEEN HAPLESS – Female, 30s to 50s. Varibald's wife.

PRINCESS POPPY – Female, 15 to early 20s. Enchanted daughter of the King and Queen.

LADY LIVIA – Female, 20s to 30s. Handmaid to the Princess.

PRINCE TRIPSALOT – Male, 20s to 30s. A young and clumsy hero who sets out to save the Princess.

SIR VALENTINE (VAL) – Male, 20s to 30s. The young valet and assistant of Prince Tripsalot.

JELLAHNDRA THE GOOD – Female, 30s to 50s. A good enchantress who helps Val and PT. (Doubled by the Queen).

LORD CHAMBERLAIN – Male, 20s to 60s. Lord under the King.

COURT JESTER – Male or Female, 20s to 40s. The Jester of the King's court.

CHORUS – Four men, four women.

PRODUCTION NOTES

GOTTA DANCE! Is based roughly on the "Twelve Dancing Princesses," with apologies to the Brothers Grimm.

Think Simple. Think suggesting an area by some small indicator. Get as elaborate or minimal as suits your taste and budget. These are just suggestions.

Act I.1. The Palace: Thrones, with brightly colored pendants or banners/ flags hung against a black backdrop or back wall. (Levels are always nice. The Royal Colors can be draped across platforms. Platforms are easily rearranged to change a scene. Scenery can be drawn and hung on them)

Act I.2. The Princess's Bedchamber. Here you will need a bed. More than that is up to you. Set dressing can consist of a few different brightly colored swaths of shiny fabric draped regally.

Act I.3. The Forest of the King. Forest décor. Change the royal silks to green. Hang them vertically against the black. Throw a real tree branch or two here and there. If you use levels, they can provide rocky slopes and such.

Act II.2. The Boat on a Magical Lake. This is explained in detail before the scene begins.

Act II.3. The Ball. Again, a palatial, elegant room can be achieved with interesting draped fabric and strings of paper lantern lights or small white Christmas lights.

General: You will need 1 slide projector and either a screen or sheet to show the slides against the back wall.

You will need to take the time to prepare the slides using your actors and props as the characters and objects projected in Act II.5.

PROPS LIST

ACT I

Assorted crowns for King, Queen, Princess, Prince
Scepter for Lord Chamberlain
Swords for Tripsalot and Valentine
Overlarge animal trap for Terrible Wretched Beast
Overlarge carpet bag for Jellahndra the Good with:
- 2 Cloaks of Invisibility
- 1 Magical Digital Mirror

Pile of worn shoes
Duck puppets – as many as needed for chorus members

ACT II

Tea pot for cocoa scene
Cups for cocoa
Vial for sleep potion in cocoa
Large sack to carry proof
Tree w/silver branches and leaves
1 twig/branch removable from tree for 'proof scene'
Golden Roses – 1 removable for 'proof scene'
Diamond Nightingales – 1 removable for 'proof scene'
Breakfast pastries for the king & queen
Slides and slide projector or PowerPoint presentation for 'proof scene'

MUSICAL NUMBERS

ACT ONE

SCENE 1 / The Palace

#1 WHAT IS HAPPENING HERE? .... Company

SCENE 2 / Princess's Bedchamber

#2 SLEEPY PRINCESS .... Princess Poppy, Lady Livia

#3 THERE'S A WORLD OUT THERE .... Lady Livia

SCENE 3 / The Forest of the King

#4 NOBLESSE OBLIGE .... Prince Tripsalot, Val the Valet

#5 NOBLESSE (Reprise) ...... Prince Tripsalot, Val the Valet & Jellahndra

SCENE 4 / The Palace

#6 SHOES .... King, Chorus

#7 OF ALL THE ROTTEN LUCK .... King, Queen & Chorus with Ducks

#8 GLORY AND HONOR .... Ensemble

ACT TWO

SCENE 1 / Princess's Bedchamber

#9 GOTTA DANCE! .... Princess Poppy, Lady Livia

#10 DON'T DRINK THE COCOA .... Company

SCENE 2 / A Boat on a Magical Lake

#11 THE MAGICAL LAKE .... Instrumental

SCENE 3 / The Ball

#12 THE BALL .... Instrumental

SCENE 4 / King's Bedchamber, The Next Morning

#13 SLEEPY PRINCESS (Reprise) .... King, Queen

SCENE 5 / The Palace, Noon of the Same Day

#14 THE MYSTERY SOLVED .... Company

#15 THERE'S A WORLD OUT THERE (Reprise-Finale) .... Company

ACT I

SCENE 1

THE PALACE OF KING VARIBALD AND QUEEN HAPLESS

#1: WHAT IS HAPPENING HERE?

LORD CHAMBERLAIN
HEY! YOU'RE PROB'LY WONDRIN' WHAT IS HAPPENIN',
WHAT IS GOING ON HERE?

CHORUS
YES, WE'VE ALL BEEN WONDRIN' WHAT IS HAPPENIN',
WHAT IS GOING ON HERE?

LORD CHAMBERLAIN
WELL, YOU SEE WE'VE GOT A REAL LIVE MYSTERY
THAT'S IN OUR KINGDOM'S HISTORY.

CHORUS
YOU SEE, IT'S QUITE A MYSTERY!

LORD CHAMBERLAIN
NOW, THE DAUGHTER OF OUR KING . . .

JESTER
. . .THE KING?

LORD CHAMBERLAIN
THE PRINCESS!

JESTER
OH, THE PRINCESS! SHE IS IN A KIND OF... THING!

LORD CHAMBERLAIN
A SPELL?!

JESTER
THAT'S IT! SHE'S IN A SPELL.

LORD CHAMBERLAIN
SO YOU'RE WONDRIN' WHAT IS GOING ON HERE.

CHORUS
WHAT IS HAPPENIN' HERE?

QUEEN
ALL SHE DOES IS SLEEP ALL DAY.

CHORUS
SHE WON'T GO OUT TO PLAY.

KING
SHE IS PALE AND WON'T EAT.

CHORUS

ALL SHE WANTS TO DO IS SLEEP.

LORD CHAMBERLAIN

SHE HAS GOT A CASE OF BLUES!

CHORUS

THE BLUES! BUT HER SHOES!
HER SHOES! HER SHOES!

Dialogue underscored.

There follows a mimed scene in which the chorus acts out this story. It can be as silly as it is magical.

KING
(spoken)

You see, a long time ago, when I was just a Prince, I met a lovely maiden.

QUEEN

Me.

KING

My Sweet Lady Hapless.

QUEEN

Me.

KING

We fell in love.

QUEEN
(aside)

Well, not at first sight. He wasn't much to look at then. But boy, could he dance!

KING

We went to every dance in the Kingdom, and back then, there were lots of them.

QUEEN

Oh we didn't go together at first. We didn't want anyone to know about us—not until we were sure.

KING

So no one knew. It seemed like chance that every night we would be at the same dance and by the end of the night we'd be dancing together. One day Hapless...

QUEEN

Me.

KING

... caught the eye of a dark Wizard. He was a very powerful Wizard. And very Evil. He wanted Hapless...

QUEEN

Me.

KING

… for himself. He tried and tried to win her.

QUEEN

Me.

KING

But by that time, we knew we were meant for one another.

QUEEN

And because love has a magic all its own…

KING

No magic the Wizard could come up with could change anything.

QUEEN

When we were married, the Wizard was furious.

KING

He promised to get even—to get revenge.

QUEEN

And when our beautiful little Princess Poppy was born, he came to her birthday party and cast a spell on her.

KING

At first we were terrified, but after a while, when we didn't notice anything unusual, we began to relax. We had a healthy, normal little Princess, and we were overjoyed.

QUEEN

But after her sixteenth birthday, things changed.

KING

We noticed that she wouldn't go out in the sunshine, or run or play.

QUEEN

She said there was no one to play with, that all her friends were frogs. Enchanted frogs!

KING

And she said she wouldn't ride her ponies anymore because they had all turned to gold! Oh, they still trotted around the fields, but they were solid gold! And you know what? It was true!

QUEEN

We knew there was some powerful magic at work!

KING

Suddenly, all the things our beloved Princess Poppy used to love to do… Well, all of a sudden, all she wanted to do was sleep!

QUEEN

All day.

KING

We'd kiss her goodnight each night, and go off to our rooms. But in the morning, when we'd come in to wake her and urge her to go out to play, she was always too tired.

QUEEN

And we found her shoes… her shoes…

KING

Her shoes…

QUEEN

Ripped to shreds,

KING

Scuffed,

QUEEN

Worn out—

KING

As if she'd been dragging them across cobbled streets.

(singing)

MANY YOUNG MEN, TRUE AND RIGHT,
THEY TRIED TO WATCH HER THROUGH THE NIGHT,
TRIED TO SEE WHERE SHE WOULD GO,
BUT WHEN THE MORNING CAME, OH, WOE!

QUEEN

ME, OH MY, I COULD JUST WEEP,
ALL THE BRAVEST FELL ASLEEP!

KING & QUEEN

OH THOSE POOR BRAVE DARING LADS!

CHORUS

OH, MY! WE COULD JUST WEEP!

LORD CHAMBERLAIN

THE ENCHANTMENT CAN…

MALE CHORUS

… IT CAN'T!

FEMALE CHORUS

IT CAN!

LORD CHAMBERLAIN

IT'LL ONLY BE REPEALED
WHEN THE EXPLOITS OF THE PRINCESS ARE REVEALED.

CHORUS

THEY HAVE BEEN REVEALED!

LORD CHAMBERLAIN
WITHOUT THE INFORMATION LEADING TO AN EXPLANATION…

CHORUS
THE WIZARD'S PENALTY FOR FAILURE IS A
HORRID TRANSFORMATION!

LORD CHAMBERLAIN
SO YOU SEE THE DAUGHTER OF OUR KING...

JESTER
... THE PRINCESS?

LORD CHAMBERLAIN
YES, THE PRINCESS!

JESTER
HAS COME UNDERNEATH A… THING…

CHORUS
… A SPELL!!

JESTER
(spoken)

I knew that!

CHORUS
OH WON'T SOMEBODY FIND OUT PLEASE,
WHERE SHE'S GOING EV'RY NIGHT, PLEASE,
WON'T SOMEBODY SET HER FREE?

KING & QUEEN
PLEASE SOMEBODY, SET US FREE!

CHORUS
WHAT IS HAPPENIN', WHAT IS HAPPENIN',
WHAT IS HAPPENIN' HERE?

SCENE 2

PRINCESS'S ROOM

PRINCESS POPPY is in bed wearing a night mask. As LADY LIVIA annoys her, she pulls the covers over her head, curls up in a ball, puts her rear in the air, generally resisting all efforts to move her. When she can resist no longer, she allows herself to be dressed, but is practically comatose during the scene, yawning, stretching, etc.

#2: SLEEPY PRINCESS

LADY LIVIA

Come on Sleepyhead. Time to wake up.

PRINCESS POPPY

Go away! Let me sleep.

LADY LIVIA

You can't keep sleeping, Princess. You're going to miss your whole life if you stay in bed.

PRINCESS POPPY

Leave me alone. I'm tired.

LADY LIVIA

Nope. Not a chance.

PRINCESS POPPY

Go away. Annoying a Princess is a capital offense.

LADY LIVIA

Not when the King and Queen have given you your orders.

PRINCESS POPPY

If you don't quit bothering me, I'll have you put in the darkest dungeon…

LADY LIVIA

Up, up, up…

PRINCESS POPPY

… with nothing to eat but bread and water…

LADY LIVIA

The New Palace Diet? I could stand to lose a few pounds.

PRINCESS POPPY

Beat it!

LADY LIVIA

(in Drill Sergeant voice)

UP! NOW!

The Princess rises and sings her lament. During the song, LADY LIVIA dresses her.

PRINCESS POPPY

IF I SLEEP ALL DAY, SLEEP THE DAY AWAY,
WHAT IS IT TO YOU, DEAR?
EXHAUSTED AS I AM, TIRED AS A LAMB,
WEARY DERRIERE HERE!
MY ARMS, THEY FEEL LIKE LEAD, ALSO DOES MY HEAD,
BOTH MY ARMS ARE BOULDERS,
MY LEGS, THEY FEEL IT TOO, ALL I WANT TO DO
IS STAY HERE IN BED.

LADY LIVIA

No, Ma'am. You can't just lie there. The sun's shining. The flowers are . . . flowering.

PRINCESS POPPY

WHAT IS ALL THE FLAP, WON'T YOU LET ME NAP?
I AM HURTING NO ONE.
I'M NOT CRAZY 'BOUT THE SUN, NOT LIKE EVERYONE
I DON'T SEE THE PROBLEM.
GO ON AND LET ME REST, GO AWAY AND 'JEST'
LEAVE ME WITH MY PILLOW.
MY COMFORTER IS BEST, COZY AS A NEST.
LEAVE ME ALONE!

LADY LIVIA

Why, look, there's a little Bluebird of Happiness on your windowsill, just waiting for you to get up and play.

PRINCESS POPPY

(fully dressed and back in bed)

I don't do birds!

(singing)

I AM SLEEPY! OH SO SLEEPY!
YOU ARE MISSING ALL THE CLUES
I AM SLEEPY! OH SO SLEEPY!
CAN'T YOU TELL I NEED MY SNOOZE?
I AM SLEEPY! OH SO SLEEPY!
IS THERE SOMEWHERE YOU SHOULD BE?
I AM SLEEPY! OH SO SLEEPY!
WOULD YOU GO AND LET ME BE?

LADY LIVIA

Okay then, there are all those cute little enchanted frogs...

PRINCESS POPPY

Frogs?!

PRINCESS POPPY (CONT'D)
(singing)
ENCHANTED FROGS HAVE JUST ONE THING ON THEIR MINDS—
COMING HERE FOR DINNER. THEY ALWAYS FREAK ME OUT,
SPREADING WARTS ABOUT, I BREAK OUT IN A FEVER.
BESIDES, I HATE THEIR GAMES, STUPID KISSING GAMES,
TURNING INTO PRINCES. HA! PRINCES, WHAT THE HECK!
THEY ALL LOOK LIKE SHREK!
LEAVE ME ALONE!

LADY LIVIA
Well then, how 'bout taking a ride on your golden pony?

PRINCESS POPPY
Have you ever ridden a golden pony?

She rubs her rear.

They're not very comfortable.
(singing)
I AM SLEEPY! OH SO SLEEPY!
YOU ARE MISSING ALL THE CLUES
I AM SLEEPY! OH SO SLEEPY!
CAN'T YOU TELL I NEED MY...

End Music.

LADY LIVIA
(cutting her off)
Listen to me, Princess. You've got to get up! Your parents are frantic. Every morning they come in and find you still in bed, your brand new shoes all ripped to shreds.

PRINCESS POPPY
You're rhyming again.

LADY LIVIA
They've hired dozens of young men to watch to find out where you go at night, but because of that stupid enchantment, they fall asleep. Then three days later, they turn into...

She can't say it.

Because of you, our little Kingdom has more farm animals per capita than any other Kingdom in the neighborhood, and there are hardly any young men left! And I MISS them.

PRINCESS POPPY
Because of ME? You're every bit as responsible. You help me. You come *with* me every night. I don't get it! Why aren't you tired? Why aren't your shoes wrecked every morning?

LADY LIVIA
I really don't know. I guess because I'm not under the same spell. I get to sleep while you...

PRINCESS POPPY
(very counter-intelligence; she looks around—the walls may have ears)

Shhh. No more words…

#3: THERE'S A WORLD OUT THERE

LADY LIVIA

Oh, Princess, please get out of bed. There's a world out there and you're missing it.

(singing)

PRINCESS, THERE'S A WORLD OUT THERE,
TIME TO RISE AND PLAY.
YOU ONLY GET ONE CHANCE, MY FRIEND.
DON'T LET IT SLIP AWAY!
COME ON AND FEEL THE SUN UPON YOUR FACE.
DON'T YOU TELL ME THAT YOU HATE TO WAKE!
AMAZING ADVENTURES WILL AWAIT YOU THERE.

IF YOU BURY YOUR OWN HEAD IN THAT COZY BED
YOU'LL BE MISSING ALL THE FUN SLUMBERING INSTEAD.
FABULOUS PLEASURES AWAIT OUTSIDE,
MAGIC CARPETS, GIANT EAGLES TO RIDE.
AMAZING ADVENTURES WILL AWAIT YOU THERE.

EVERY MORNING FINDS YOU SNORING
STILL BENEATH YOUR PILLOW.
THE WORLD IS WAITING JUST OUTSIDE YOUR COVERS.

PRINCESS POPPY

Go away!

LADY LIVIA

COME ON, POPPY, NOW.
PRINCESS, THERE'S A WORLD OUT THERE.
YOU ONLY GET ONE CHANCE.
TIME TO WAKE UP, TIME TO GO, TIME TO FIND ROMANCE.
TRAVEL ON TO LONDON, ROME, BOMBAY!
JUST DO SOMETHING. DON'T LET LIFE SLIP AWAY!
AMAZING ADVENTURES STILL AWAIT YOU THERE!

FROM GOLD SWINGS THAT GRANT WISHES,
FLYING FISH THAT CROON TUNES,
TO THE TREES GROWING BONBONS
IN THE CHOCOLATE LAGOON,
YOU'LL MISS ALL OF THE WONDER
LYING THERE IN YOUR BED,

LADY LIVIA (CONT'D)
HIDING IN YOUR BLANKET COCOON!

PRINCESS, THERE'S A WORLD OUT THERE.
YOU ONLY GET ONE CHANCE.
TIME TO WAKE UP, TIME TO GO! TIME TO FIND ROMANCE!
TRAVEL TO NEW YORK, THE ALPS, OR PAREE
JUST DO SOMETHING! WAKE UP, MY FRIEND AND YOU'LL SEE,
AMAZING ADVENTURES STILL AWAIT YOU THERE!

AMAZING ADVENTURES STILL AWAIT YOU THERE!
STILL AWAIT YOU THERE!
STILL AWAIT YOU THERE!
STILL AWAIT YOU THERE!

LADY LIVIA pushes a groggy PRINCESS POPPY out the door of her room as the scene changes to a forest not too far from the castle.

SCENE 3

IN THE FOREST OF THE KING

A road outside of town. From behind a tree or off sight lines, comes a terrible moaning and groaning—a fierce racket.

PRINCE TRIPSALOT (OFFSTAGE)

I heard that noise over here. This way.

PRINCE TRIPSALOT (PT) enters and trips over nothing. He trips often, mostly over his own feet. PT is followed by SIR VALENTINE.

VALENTINE

Be careful PT. I don't like the way it sounds. It sounds big and scary.

PRINCE TRIPSALOT

I'm not afraid, Val. I'm one of the good guys.

VALENTINE

Yeah, I know, but…

PRINCE TRIPSALOT

No buts about it.

VALENTINE

Listen, PT, my job is to see that you're okay. Your mother and father, the King and Queen of Benson Beyond the River, would be very upset with me if I let you get into trouble.

PRINCE TRIPSALOT

Let me? Let me? You can't stop me. I'm perfectly capable of getting into trouble all by myself.

VALENTINE

I KNOW! That's what I mean. It's like you're a trouble magnet. My job is to keep you from finding it before it finds you.

PRINCE TRIPSALOT

Well, you can't, and if you want to stay my best friend, then you've got to back off and let me get into my own messes. *Noblesse Oblige*!

VALENTINE

Wha?

PRINCE TRIPSALOT

Noblesse Oblige! The obligation of the noble to help the less fortunate.

VALENTINE

That's the craziest thing I ever heard of.

PRINCE TRIPSALOT

That's because you're not a nobleman. I am. I am a potential hero. If there's a mess somewhere, I MUST step up. I MUST be brave.

PRINCE TRIPSALOT (CONT'D)
(holding up a finger)

Me.

(holding up a different finger)

Mess. We're like this!

He tries to cross his fingers, but his hands get twisted.

VALENTINE

I know. I know. But it's me who has to get you OUT of the messes.

Moaning and groaning again.

PRINCE TRIPSALOT

Shh. I hear it again. Over this way.

VALENTINE

PT... Please. Let's get out of this forest. I don't like it. It feels spooky. We shouldn't even be here, this far away from home.

#4: NOBLESSE OBLIGE

PRINCE TRIPSALOT

A prince can't stay at home all his life. A prince is meant to go out into the world and have adventures. You know, undertake heroic quests, defeat dragons, win princesses. You know. You've read the same books I have.

(singing)

SIR GAWAIN, ST. GEORGE, AND KING ARTHUR OF YORE,
HAD INSTRUCTIONS PASSED DOWN FROM
THEIR FATHERS BEFORE.
IT'S *NOBLESSE OBLIGE*, VAL, AND I'VE GOT IT TOO.
FOR THIS IS WHAT I'M BORN TO DO.

VALENTINE

Don't hurt yourself!

PRINCE TRIPSALOT

A PRINCE CAN'T STAY HOME FOR THE REST OF HIS LIFE
HE'S GOT TO BE DARING, AND FACE ALL THE STRIFE.
HE'S GOT TO BE BRAVE, AND HE'S GOT TO BE TRUE.

VALENTINE

In short, he must be more like you.

PRINCE TRIPSALOT

You've got it!

VALENTINE

Yeah, PT, that's all well and good, but I promised your folks I'd look after you! PT? Hello?

Ignoring him, PT continues to sing.

PRINCE TRIPSALOT

WHETHER I'M QUESTING OR SEEKING THE GRAIL
CONQUERING ARMIES OR SAVING THE GIRL,
WHETHER I'M SLAYING A DRAGON OR TWO,
IT'S SOMETHING THAT I'VE GOT TO DO.

VALENTINE

Whatever.

PRINCE TRIPSALOT

I MAY NOT BE HANDSOME, I MAY NOT BE BRIGHT,
IT'S TRUE THAT I'M CLUMSY AND SOMETIMES A SIGHT,
BUT MY HEART IS HONEST, MY MOTIVES ARE PURE,
I'M REALLY A NICE GUY, FOR SURE. I MEAN IT.
GALAHAD, LANCELOT, CHARMING OR SHREK,
ALL WERE OBLIGED THEN TO RISK THEIR OWN NECKS,
IT'S *NOBLESSE OBLIGE*, VAL, AND I'VE GOT IT TOO.
THIS IS WHAT I'M BORN TO DO.

VALENTINE

Sounds more like a disease to me.

PRINCE TRIPSALOT

Val, there's important work to be done!

(singing)

A SPELL OF ENCHANTMENT HAS COVERED THE LAND,
A MYSTERY CONJURED BY THE DARK WIZARD'S HAND.
THE KING HAS DECREED THAT A PRINCE SHOULD GO FORTH,
MY BROTHERS WERE BUSY. . .

VALENTINE

... Of course! So you're it.

PRINCE TRIPSALOT

POPPY'S ENCHANTMENT HAS HER PARENTS CONFUSED.
SHE'S GOT HER DAYS BACKWARDS,
SHE'S WRECKING HER SHOES.
I'LL FIND OUT HER SECRET AND HELP HER GET WELL.
IT'S SOMETHING THAT I'VE GOT TO DO.
CAN'T YOU TELL?
WHETHER I'M QUESTING OR SEEKING THE GRAIL
CONQUERING ARMIES OR SAVING THE GIRL,
WHETHER I'M SLAYING A DRAGON OR THREE,
IT'S *NOBLESSE OBLIGE.* NOW YOU SEE!

(spoken)

Join me, Val!

PRINCE TRIPSALOT & VALENTINE

WHETHER WE'RE QUESTING OR SEEKING THE GRAIL
CONQUERING ARMIES OR SAVING THE GIRL,

PRINCE TRIPSALOT & VALENTINE (CONT'D)

WHETHER WE'RE SLAYING A DRAGON OR THREE

PRINCE TRIPSALOT

IT'S NOBLESSE OBLIGE! NOW FOR ME.

(spoken)

One more time!

PRINCE TRIPSALOT & VALENTINE

WHETHER WE'RE QUESTING OR SEEKING THE GRAIL
CONQUERING ARMIES OR SAVING THE GIRL,
WHETHER WE'RE SLAYING A DRAGON OR THREE

PRINCE TRIPSALOT

IT'S NOBLESSE OBLIGE!

VALENTINE

SAY, I'M SAVING THE DAY!

PRINCE TRIPSALOT & VALENTINE

HEY! IT'S *NOBLESSE OBLIGE* NOW FOR ME!

(spoken)

It's Noblesse Oblige!

VALENTINE

Yeah, but this is too scary. This forest has weird things going on. Did you see that tree back there? There were no leaves on it, just little round... uh... weird things.

PRINCE TRIPSALOT

They smelled so sweet, good enough to eat. Why'd you have to knock me down? I really wanted to try one of those things.

VALENTINE

Are you crazy? No offense, but they might have been poison!

PRINCE TRIPSALOT

Well, they sure looked good enough to eat.

(dreamily)

You shouldn't have knocked my hand. I bet they were candy.

VALENTINE

Not a chance. Besides, what if when you ate one, and you suddenly fell into a 100-year sleep? Or got turned into a toad or an enchanted mushroom? What would I tell your mom and dad then? Huh? Huh? And even if it was candy, candy rots your teeth.

PRINCE TRIPSALOT

(still dreamily)

Remember that lagoon we passed? I could swear it was made out of cocoa. It sure smelled like cocoa. I love cocoa... especially hot, at night, right before bed, with lotsa little marshmallows floating on the top. Mmmm.

VALENTINE

I tell you, something's not right here!

PRINCE TRIPSALOT

Whatever... We're here in this forest...

VALENTINE

This very, very WEIRD forest...

PRINCE TRIPSALOT

We're here in this forest because this is the only way to get to King Varibald's Kingdom. And I must...

(very Superhero-like)

... undertake the challenge to find out what enchantment the princess is under.

VALENTINE

(gloom & doom)

But PT, the penalty for failure is some kind of hideous transformation...

PRINCE TRIPSALOT

I DON'T intend to fail. Besides, I am fearless. I am dauntless. I am courage personified.

Moaning/groaning again. PT trips and falls in terror.

AAAAAAAAA?

VALENTINE

It's getting closer! Let's get out of here.

PRINCE TRIPSALOT

Cut it out, Val. I was momentarily startled. There. It's coming from there.

By this time, the TERRIBLE WRETCHED BEAST caught in a snare has pulled itself onto the stage. The two young men approach. The TWB is in obvious agony, snapping at them as they try to get closer.

Look, Val. The poor thing is caught in a trap.

VALENTINE

Let's get out of here. That thing looks like it could do some serious damage if it got loose.

PRINCE TRIPSALOT

(ignoring him, and focused on the TWB)

There, there, fella.

Throughout the next speeches, TWB reacts with appropriate snarling, growling, snapping and such.

Don't be afraid. I'm not going to hurt you.

VALENTINE

Come away from there before it bites your hand off. Or worse!

TWB

Roar.

PRINCE TRIPSALOT

I'm Prince Tripsalot, and this is my buddy Val. He's my best friend.

VALENTINE

Come away, I tell you. Leave the thing alone.

PRINCE TRIPSALOT

He's a little overprotective, but it's only because he likes me. I'm a very likeable guy.

TWB

Growl. Snap.

PRINCE TRIPSALOT

I wouldn't hurt you at all under any circumstances. In fact, if you let me, I'll try to help you get out of that nasty trap.

VALENTINE

Are you nuts? What happens if you let it out? It EATS us! That's what happens. We're dead! Get it? D-E-A-D! *Dead*!

PRINCE TRIPSALOT

I hate traps and I hate the people who use them. There's plenty of food at the market. There's no reason to use these cruel devices on poor unsuspecting furry little animals. Such as yourself.

TWB

Roar. Growl. Snap.

VALENTINE

PT, DON'T!!!!

PRINCE TRIPSALOT

Val, come here, I need you to hold this, so I can release the thingie…

VALENTINE

No way!

PRINCE TRIPSALOT

Val! Get over here. This poor creature is suffering. I can't stand to see it in pain.

VALENTINE

Oh, okay. You're right. Nothing should be left in that much pain, but when we release it, get ready to run like the wind, okay?

PRINCE TRIPSALOT

Why?

VALENTINE

Why? Because it looks fast. We have to be able to outrun it.

PRINCE TRIPSALOT

Actually, I only have to outrun you.

VALENTINE

Very funny!

PRINCE TRIPSALOT

Okay. Just come over here and help me.

He does. They successfully release the creature from the trap.

There now. You're free!

The Beast stands up - ominously tall – like a mother bear about to hug them in a Bear-hug of Death. Both boys back away, fall down, cower.

Then, an amazing transformation occurs. Out of the bear-suit comes Jellahndra, the Good, a woman with great magical powers. She continues toward the two men and hugs them each in turn. They babble incoherently.

TWB

Thank you, kind Sirs. You have saved me from the Dark Wizard. It was he who turned me into the pitiful howling creature you saw, trapped by the Jaws of Enchantment. Only when someone came along who was kind and brave enough to set me free would I be returned to my true form. Also, it was hot and itchy in that disgusting bear suit... and the bugs! You wouldn't believe! Thank you. Thank you. Thank you.

VALENTINE

Dark Wizard? Dark Wizard? Does that mean we have a Dark Wizard after us, now?

TWB

No, no, no, no. You see, I am Jellahndra the Good, Protectress of all of these lands. The Dark Wizard's powers won't work here while I'm around.

VALENTINE

If that's true, how come you were in his trap?

TWB

(very melodramatic)

I, Jellahndra the Good, Server of the Faithful, was tricked by the Evil One and trapped in that vicious snare... er... .

(snapping out of the melodrama and getting real)

I guess I wasn't paying attention, and POW! He nailed me. Oooo, I'm gonna get him for that! Anyway, with me tied up, so to speak, that left him free to work his evil magic and kept me from protecting this Kingdom. Now that you've released me, however, his powers are gone. In fact, with my help, all his nasty little enchantments can be undone.

VALENTINE

All his enchantments?

He looks around suspiciously.

PRINCE TRIPSALOT

Did he make the trees turn into candy and the lagoon into cocoa?

TWB

Well, actually, no. Those were mine. I have a bit of a sweet tooth. But he's the one responsible for the spell on the Princess, and all those poor young lads who tried to save her.

PRINCE TRIPSALOT

You know about that spell?

TWB

Of course. I know everything about that spell. Including how to remove it!

PRINCE TRIPSALOT

Wow! That's terrific. We're on our way to the Palace now, to volunteer to watch the Princess and see where she goes at night. Will you come along and help us?

TWB

Oh, that's sweet. You're sweet, but no, I can't come with you. I have a lot of work to do here in the forest. There are frogs to disenchant and golden ponies to make real again. Instead, I will give you three magical assists to help you be successful in your quest... But only if you use them exactly as I instruct you to.

She reaches into her bag and removes a clear plastic rain poncho.

First, I'll give you the Cloak of Invisibility…

PRINCE TRIPSALOT

But there are two of us!

TWB

Picky, Picky, Picky. All right…

She takes out another.

TWB (CONT'D)

… two cloaks of invisibility for the price of one. Next, take this Magical Digital Mirror.

She gets a large hand mirror from her bag.

It uses technology that won't be around for a thousand years yet. Just hold the mirror up to what you want to capture, like this, press this button, like this, and voila! You have an image of what you've just seen. Pretty cool, huh? But be very sure the flash function isn't on, for if it is, and it flashes, even under your cloak of invisibility, the flash will be seen.

VALENTINE

That's two. What's the third assist?

TWB

Just a piece of very valuable advice. When the Princess and her handmaiden, the Lovely Lady Livia, come to you before bedtime with a cup of cocoa, only pretend to drink it. DO NOT DRINK THE COCOA. If you do, your fate will be the same as those poor schnooks who failed to discover the Princess's secret.

PRINCE TRIPSALOT

And if we succeed?

TWB

The Princess will be freed from her enchantment and the Kingdom will once again thrive!

PRINCE TRIPSALOT

Will the princes and knights who quested before me also be restored?

TWB

Nope. Sorry. They took their chances fair and square and, sad to say, now the price they have to pay. Some things even I can't change.

PRINCE TRIPSALOT

Thank you, Jellahndra. We'll do what you say. Come on Val. Let's go to the Palace. Val? Val? Where are you?

Val has gotten into his Invisibility Cloak – just trying it on – and now he comes out to say…

VALENTINE

Wow! This is great! You really couldn't see me, huh? WOW! Think of all the fun we can have with these!

PRINCE TRIPSALOT

Give me that. Come on. This isn't supposed to be fun! We're on a heroic quest to rescue a Princess from an enchantment. Let's go!

#5: NOBLESSE (REPRISE)

We've got work to do.

PRINCE TRIPSALOT & VALENTINE

WHETHER WE'RE QUESTING OR SEEKING THE GRAIL
CONQUERING ARMIES OR SAVING THE GIRL,
WHETHER WE'RE SLAYING A DRAGON OR THREE
IT'S NOBLESSE OBLIGE!

JELLAHNDRA

HEY, YOU'RE SAVING THE DAY!

PRINCE TRIPSALOT & VALENTINE

YEAH!

ALL THREE

IT'S *NOBLESSE OBLIGE* NOW FOR ME!

THEY exit.

SCENE 4

THE PALACE

In the Palace, the **KING**, *the* **QUEEN** *and the entire court is gloomy. As the scene begins, they sing a bluesy lament.*

#6: SHOES

KING

OH, WOE IS ME, I'M WEARY. OH, BABY, BABY, CAN'T YOU SEE,
WHAT YOUR WEIRDO HABITS ARE DOING TO ME?
WE'VE GONE TO EVERYBODY,
TRIED ALL THE MAJOR SHOE DESIGNS,
FROM SAM & LIBBY, JOAN & DAVID AND BOTH THE KLEINS

(spoken)

That's Anne & Calvin.

(singing)

WE'VE PURCHASED BY THE CARTFULS
AND BY THE GROSS FROM RALPH LAUREN,
FROM K-MART, WAL-MART AND LIZ CLAY-BOREN,
FILENE'S AND MACY'S, OFF OR ON-LINE,
COLE-HAHN, KEN COLE, IT MAKES NO NEVER MIND.

CHORUS

DOLCE & GABBANA, CAPEZIO AND PRADA,
ETIENE ANGIER, AND JIMMY CHOU–

KING

BUT NADA!
NIGHT AFTER NIGHT DEAR POPPY,
YOU RUIN EACH AND EVERY PAIR.
AND EVERYONE IN THE KINGDOM IS IN DESPAIR!
OH, WOE IS ME, I'M WEARY. OH, BABY, BABY, CAN'T YOU SEE,
WHAT YOUR WEIRDO HABITS DO TO ME?

CHORUS

DOLCE & GABBANA,

KING

(spoken in Elvis-like testimonial)

That's right, Honey!

CHORUS

CAPEZIO AND PRADA,

KING

You got it, Baby!

CHORUS

ETIENE ANGIER, JIMMY CHOO–OO

KING

BUT NADA!
NIGHT AFTER NIGHT MY POPPY,
YOU RUIN EACH AND EVERY PAIR.
AND EVERYONE BUT THE SHOEMAKERS ARE IN DESPAIR!
OH, WOE IS ME, I'M WEARY. OH, BABY, BABY, CAN'T YOU SEE,
WHAT YOUR WEIRDO HABITS DO TO ME?

(spoken)

I'll tell you one more time!

(singing)

WHAT YOUR WEIRDO HABITS DO TO ME?

(spoken a-la 'Elvis')

That's all. Thank you, thank you very much.

More gloom and doom as PRINCE TRIPSALOT and VALENTINE enter and approach the KING and QUEEN.

PRINCE TRIPSALOT

(bowing)

Your Majesties. I am Prince Benson Edgar Allagar Wilfurness Tripsalot, heir to the Kingdom of Benson Beyond the River. My father, the King and my mother the Queen, send their regards and their deep regrets about your great misfortune.

QUEEN

Thank you, Prince... ? Er... that's a pretty long name.

KING

Yes. What shall we call you? After all, we can't just call you Prince. It would sound like we were calling a German shepherd!

PRINCE TRIPSALOT

Just call me PT. Prince Tripsalot. PT. Get it?

KING

(doubtful)

Tripsalot?

PRINCE TRIPSALOT

It is my father's name and was my grandfather's and my great-grandfather's and my great-great-grandfather's and my great-great-great-grandfather's and my...

VALENTINE

(thumps him)

They get it, PT!

PRINCE TRIPSALOT

Well, there's this long history of stumbling in our family. It's passed down from generation to generation through the male line. All the men in our family have it.

He trips over his own feet.

PRINCE TRIPSALOT (CONT'D)
(smiling sheepishly)

I got it too.

During the scene, a flirtation begins between LADY LIVIA and VALENTINE, all mime, and VERY obvious. VALENTINE is definitely NOT paying attention to the warnings.

KING

What brings you to our Kingdom, PT?

PRINCE TRIPSALOT

Noblesse Oblige.

KING

Gesundheit!

PRINCE TRIPSALOT

Noblesse Oblige. Noblesse Oblige!

KING

Sorry?

PRINCE TRIPSALOT

The obligation of the nobility.

KING
(not getting it at all)

Oh.

PRINCE TRIPSALOT

I heard about the Princess's enchantment...

He sees PRINCESS POPPY for the first time. PRINCESS is drowsing against LADY LIVIA. Every now and then she startles awake, like someone sleeping on a subway train, snorts, snuffles, then falls back to sleep.

(clearly smitten)

... wow! Anyway, I heard Princess Poppy somehow manages to wear out her shoes every night even though she never seems to leave the palace. It's a mystery that clearly needs a heroic solution, and I'm just the hero to figure it out.

QUEEN

Oh, but my dear PT, there's a dreadful penalty for those who try and fail.

PRINCE TRIPSALOT

Nothing could be worse than the penalty for a Prince who doesn't try. I couldn't live with myself if I didn't at least try.

KING

But if you try and fail, you might not *want* to live with yourself! You really should hear the conditions before you sign your name to the contract. Once you've signed your name, there's no turning back.

VALENTINE

(temporarily drawn back into the conversation)

Conditions? What are the conditions?

PRINCE TRIPSALOT

No conditions could change my mind.

VAL is quickly distracted once again by LADY LIVIA.

KING

You and your friend...

PRINCE TRIPSALOT

Sir Val.

KING

... Sir Val, will wait in a chamber just inside the Princess's locked, bolted and barricaded room. You must keep watch all night to be sure the Princess doesn't slip out.

PRINCE TRIPSALOT

Her room is bolted and locked?

KING

And barricaded. From the outside!

PRINCE TRIPSALOT

And there are no other entrances, exits or secret passages in that room?

KING

That's correct. None!

PRINCE TRIPSALOT

And we will be INSIDE the room?

KING

That's right.

PRINCE TRIPSALOT

Then what?

KING

If she should somehow escape the locked room with its many locks, bolts and barricades, it will be your job to follow her, to learn where she goes and why her shoes are always destroyed in the morning.

QUEEN

You'll need to bring back proof of where she goes. Otherwise, it will be just your word against hers.

KING

"He says, she says."

PRINCE TRIPSALOT

Okay and then what?

KING

In the morning, you must come before the entire court and report your findings. The Princess must agree that you are telling the truth. If you fail, you will be transformed, like all the others.

PRINCE TRIPSALOT

Okay with me. Where do I sign?

QUEEN

Wait! Before you sign, remember that it's irreversible.

KING

Once your name is on this paper, your transformation, should you fail, can never be reversed.

PRINCE TRIPSALOT

Never?

KING

Never.

PRINCE TRIPSALOT

And if I succeed?

KING

If you do succeed, your reward will be generous. For your part in ending this dilemma, I'll give you half my lands, half my wealth and all of my gratitude forever and ever more.

PRINCE TRIPSALOT

Excuse me, Sire. If it's all right with you, Majesties, I'd like one thing more?

KING

One thing more?

PRINCE TRIPSALOT

Yes. Well, it's just... er... even asleep, I can see that your daughter is lovely to look at. And, while, I don't know her, of course, if I do succeed, I'd like permission to remain in your Kingdom for awhile. I'd like to have a chance to get to know the Princess better. Maybe, if she likes me... I mean... if we like each other... if we have things we like to do together, if we have things to talk about together... well... we might... like... you know... join our two Kingdoms some day?

KING

That's a terrific idea, PT. You seem like a really nice, if clumsy, kinda guy. So, yes. It's all right with me. Of course, we'll have to ask the Princess. We'll ask her as soon as she wakes up.

PRINCE TRIPSALOT

Okay then, where do I sign?

QUEEN

Oh, PT, it's not wise for you to sign so quickly. You really should hear about all the others...

ALL

Yes, you really should hear about all the others...

QUEEN

Yes, go on. Tell him. Tell him all... the horrible, terrible truth...

KING

You tell him, Dear.

QUEEN

No, you tell him.

KING

No, you.

QUEEN

No, you.

KING

No, you.

QUEEN

No, you.

KING

No, you.

LORD CHAMBERLAIN

Oh, for goodness sakes! Won't somebody tell him!!

QUEEN

Oh, all right! I'll tell him.

#7: OF ALL THE ROTTEN LUCK

(singing)

THEY ALL CAME FROM MILES AROUND, THE INNOCENTS...

KING

... THE JERKS!

QUEEN

THEY SIGNED THE KING'S AGREEMENT,
THEN THEY EACH SET OUT TO WORK.
BUT EVERY ONE, YES EVERY ONE,
THEY SLEPT THE NIGHT AWAY,
OH, YES, OH, YES, THEY SLEPT THE NIGHT AWAY.

KING

SO THEY TRAVELED BACK TO THEIR HOMES,
IN DISGRACE, IN SHAME
AND BEFORE THREE DAYS WERE OUT,
THE TRANSFORMATION CAME.

Music underscores testimonials.

SPOKEN #1

Of all the rotten luck, I used to have a handsome son, but, woe is me, for now I have a duck.

SPOKEN #2

He doesn't even lay eggs!

SPOKEN #3

We can't have him for Sunday dinner!

SPOKEN #2

Eeeeooou.

SPOKEN #4

Mine can't even swim! Who ever heard of a duck that can't swim?

SPOKEN #1

Just three short days after he got back,
All he could ever say to us was, 'Quack.'

SPOKEN #2

My son was dashing, young and plucky,
Now he's replaced my rubber ducky.

SPOKEN #3

Our Jack was searching for his Jill,
But now just 'quacks' come from his bill.

SPOKEN #4

He used to wear Italian leathers.
Now he's sporting yellow feathers.

CHORUS

DOES YOUR MOTHER KNOW? DOES YOUR FATHER AGREE?
ARE YOU SURE YOU WANT THIS MISSION?
WHAT IS HAPPENIN' HERE IS JUST AWFUL YOU SEE,
THAT YOU DIDN'T SIGN UP YOU'LL BE A-WISHIN'.
BE CAREFUL WHAT YOU WISH FOR
AND ALWAYS BE SURE YOU KNOW
THE PRICE FOR YOUR NOBLESSE OBLIGE.

PRINCE TRIPSALOT

IT SOUNDS A *FOWL* WAY TO SPEND YOUR LIFE, QUACKING!

CHORUS

BUT THAT'S THE PRICE YOU'LL HAVE TO PAY!

CHORUS (CONT'D)
THAT'S THE PRICE YOU'LL PAY TODAY!

VALENTINE
So, PT, what's the deal?

PRINCE TRIPSALOT
Didn't you hear?

VALENTINE
(glancing at Lady Livia)
I was kind of… distracted. So tell me. What's in it for us besides *Noblesse Oblige*?

PRINCE TRIPSALOT
Excuse me, your Majesty, but could you tell my Valet once more what your reward is for solving this mystery?

KING
Starting from… where?

VALENTINE
Um… from "What brings you to this Kingdom?"

KING
Oh dear. Well, let me put it to you this way... Lord Chamberlain, if you please.

#8: GLORY AND HONOR

LORD CHAMBERLAIN
POWER AND RICHES AND FAME AND A CHANCE FOR WINNING
GLORY AND HONOR AND MORE
WEALTH BEYOND YOUR DREAMS YOU CAN'T IGNORE
DIAMONDS AND JEWELS AND CASTLES WITH SUITS OF ARMOR
SERVANTS AND GUARDS AT YOUR DOOR
WILL BE GIVEN YOU FOREVERMORE

KING
IF YOU'LL JUST FOLLOW THE PRINCESS THROUGH THE NIGHT
AND FIND OUT WHERE HER FLIGHT TRULY TAKES HER,
IF YOU CAN SOLVE THE MYSTERY OF HER SHOES
THEN I WILL GIVE TO YOU ALL THIS AND MORE

CHORUS
POWER AND RICHES AND FAME AND A CHANCE FOR WINNING
GLORY AND HONOR, OH MY!
WEALTH BEYOND YOUR DREAMS YOU CAN'T DENY!

PRINCE TRIPSALOT
BUT DIAMONDS AND JEWELS ARE NOT OUR REWARD FOR TRYING
HELPING THE KING IS OUR PRIZE.
SOME THINGS WE MUST JUST DO BECAUSE IT IS RIGHT

VALENTINE

LET'S GET THIS STRAIGHT; IF WE BOTH SIT AND WAIT
UNTIL IT'S VERY LATE, IN HER BEDROOM,
AND FIGURE OUT WHERE AND HOW SHE GETS ABOUT,
OUR REWARD'S JUST "MORAL" CLOUT?

PRINCE TRIPSALOT

WELL, THAT'S THE PLAN

VALENTINE

(to the King)

He's your man!

PRINCE TRIPSALOT

NOBLESSE OBLIGE, VAL, THAT'S THE REASON
WE ARE ON THIS QUEST,
HELPING THESE DAMSELS IN DISTRESS.
WEALTH BEYOND OUR DREAMS IS DOING WHAT'S BEST!
YOU MAY WIN THE ONE YOU ADORE . . .

VALENTINE

You mean the Lady Livia?!

PRINCE TRIPSALOT

WHY NOT? THE WORLD'S AT OUR DOOR!
SHE WILL HONOR YOU FOREVERMORE!

KING

OH, BY THE WAY, YOU CAN'T JUST SIT AND PLAY,
THE PENALTY TO STRAY FROM YOUR MISSION
IS QUITE SEVERE; IN THREE DAYS YOU'LL APPEAR
IN FEATHERS AND A BILL
YOU'LL BOTH BE DUCKS!

VALENTINE

What the . . . ?

DUCKS (CHORUS)

"QUACK!"

CHORUS

... GOOD LUCK!

(under following dialogue)

POWER AND RICHES AND FAME AND A CHANCE FOR WINNING
GLORY AND HONOR AND MORE
WEALTH BEYOND YOUR DREAMS YOU CAN'T IGNORE

DIAMONDS AND JEWELS AND CASTLES WITH SUITS OF ARMOR
SERVANTS AND GUARDS AT YOUR DOOR
WEALTH BEYOND YOUR DREAMS YOU CAN'T IGNORE
DIAMONDS AND JEWELS AND CASTLES WITH SUITS OF ARMOR
SERVANTS AND GUARDS AT YOUR DOOR

VALENTINE

I don't know. Maybe we'd better think this through again. I'm allergic to feathers!

PRINCE TRIPSALOT

Have you forgotten our magical help from Jellahndra?

VALENTINE

Nooo, but how do we know those things will work? What if they don't work?

PRINCE TRIPSALOT

You tried on the Cloak of Invisibility. I couldn't see you!

VALENTINE

True.

PRINCE TRIPSALOT

And we have the Magic Digital Mirror to bring back proof!

VALENTINE

True. But what if the Princess says we made it all up?

PRINCE TRIPSALOT

Princesses don't lie.

VALENTINE

Well...

He spots Lady Livia, and the attraction between them is very obvious.

PRINCE TRIPSALOT

Then, if you have no more objections, I'm going to sign us up. Come on, Val, it'll be a great adventure.

PT trips on his way to sign the contract. VALENTINE is still not convinced.

CHORUS

WE WILL HONOR YOU FOREVER . . .

VALENTINE

... WE'LL BE IN DUCK SOUP TOGETHER!

CHORUS

... WE WILL HONOR YOU FOREVERMORE!

PRINCE TRIPSALOT

We're in!

VALENTINE

... We're not!

PRINCE TRIPSALOT

We're in!

VALENTINE

... We're not!

PRINCE TRIPSALOT

We're in!

CHORUS

HOORAY!

VALENTINE
(to audience)

NOT!

END OF ACT ONE

ACT II

SCENE 1

THE PRINCESS'S BEDCHAMBER

The Princess's bedchamber is divided by a privacy screen. The 'watchers' are unlit but already in place on one side, the women are in light on the other. The PRINCESS and LADY LIVIA are dressing for an evening out. Livia is laying out the Princess's clothes.

#9: GOTTA DANCE

PRINCESS POPPY

GOTTA DANCE, I GOTTA!
OH, THERE'S NOTHIN' GONNA KEEP ME AT HOME.
FOR WHEN THE SUN GOES DOWN AND THE MOON COMES OUT
MY FEET BOTH HAVE A MIND OF THEIR OWN.

BECAUSE I GOTTA DANCE, YES SIR, I GOTTA DANCE.
THE WHOLE THING'S OUT OF MY CONTROL.
SO OFF TO THE MAGICAL BALL I GO!

WHIRLING, TWIRLING, SPINNING,
DANCING ALL THROUGH THE NIGHT,
DRESSED IN GOWNS OF GOLD AND SILVER WHILE
HANDSOME PARTNERS HOLD ME OH, SO TIGHT!

AND WE JUST GOTTA DANCE, OH YES, WE GOTTA DANCE.
WHY SIT AROUND AND WAIT TO GROW OLD?
WHEN I CAN GET ON THAT FLOOR AND GO!

THEY SAY THAT I AM UNDER A SPELL,
WELL, EVEN IF THAT IS TRUE.
I'LL DO WHAT I HAVE TO DO, BECAUSE I'VE GOTTA DANCE
I GOTTA GET UP AND DANCE!

Instrumental music for dance routine.

PRINCESS POPPY & LADY LIVIA

WHIRLING, TWIRLING, SPINNING, DANCING
ALL THROUGH THE NIGHT,
DRESSED IN GOWNS OF GOLD AND SILVER WHILE
HANDSOME PARTNERS HOLD US OH, SO TIGHT!

AND WE JUST GOTTA DANCE, OH YES, WE GOTTA DANCE.
WHY SIT AROUND AND WAIT TO GROW OLD?
WHEN WE CAN GET ON THAT FLOOR AND GO!

PRINCESS POPPY & LADY LIVIA (CONT'D)

THEY SAY THAT WE ARE UNDER A SPELL,
WELL, EVEN IF THAT IS TRUE.
WE'LL DO WHAT WE HAVE TO DO,
BECAUSE WE'VE GOTTA DANCE
WE GOTTA GET UP AND DANCE!

By the end of the song, the Princess is fully dressed in a ball gown with a bathrobe over it. Her fancy shoes, however, can be seen under the robe. LADY LIVIA is also dressed for an evening's outing. THEY prepare the drugged cocoa for the two would-be heroes.

LADY LIVIA

I reeeallly hate to do this.

PRINCESS POPPY

What's wrong with you? I've never seen you like this.

LADY LIVIA

They really seem nice.

PRINCESS POPPY

Nonsense. They're just like all the others. All they want is half my father's Kingdom and a lot of gold and jewels. Heroes! They're all alike. Half the Kingdom, pots of wealth. There are even some Kings who offer their daughter the Princess's hand in marriage as payment in one of these quest things they do! Can you imagine? What are we, property?

LADY LIVIA

These two seem like awfully sweet guys. The Prince asked if he could stay around the Kingdom after…

PRINCESS POPPY

Not convinced.

LADY LIVIA

… to get to know you better. I don't think he's just after the pots of wealth, Princess Poppy. He's got his own Kingdom. Why would he need yours?

PRINCESS POPPY

Well. I do like how he falls down a lot. That's sort of sweet. But… No. We've got to go through with it.

LADY LIVIA

The Prince's man, Val…

She flutters a little when she says his name.

… seems awfully nice. I just love the way the tip of his nose turns up in that cute little way.

PRINCESS POPPY

What? Since when have you been interested in noses? This is so unlike you, Livia. You're worrying me.

LADY LIVIA

I know. I just hate to see two such eligible… I mean, it's such a waste!

(lamenting)

We have enough ducks!

PRINCESS POPPY

Listen…

Her feet start to move without her willing them to. She's beginning to feel the enchantment.

I can't wait much longer. We're running out of time. Mix up the sleeping draft. Then we can get out of here.

#10: DON'T DRINK THE COCOA

LADY LIVIA

I'm not happy about this, Princess.

PRINCESS POPPY

(not mean, just frantic)

You don't have to be happy! I'm the Princess. *I* have to be happy. Now, just DO IT!

VALENTINE photographs LADY LIVIA & PRINCESS POPPY as they drug the cocoa.

(singing)

HURRY UP, GIRL! IT'S ALMOST TIME TO GO.
THE BOAT IS WAITING FOR US DOWN BELOW.
MIX UP THAT COCOA WITH THE SLEEPING POTION
AND FLOAT SOME MARSHMALLOWS ON THE CHOCOLATE OCEAN.

The Magic Digital Mirror is seen above the screen. It takes a picture of the girls drugging the cocoa.

LADY LIVIA

OH, PRINCESS, PRINCESS, I HATE TO DO IT.
OH, PRINCESS, PRINCESS, WE'RE GONNA RUE IT.

PRINCESS POPPY

HURRY UP, GIRL, FOR WE'VE GOT TO GO!
THE BOAT IS WAITING FOR US DOWN BELOW.

Meanwhile, on the other side of the screen…

VALENTINE

Did you see how Lady Livia looked at me? She likes me. I know she does.

PRINCE TRIPSALOT

You're a very likeable guy.

VALENTINE

No! I mean, *likes* me. You know boy, girl, boyfriend, girlfriend? That kind of *likes* me.

PRINCE TRIPSALOT

Ohhh! I don't think I've ever seen you *that* interested in a girl before.

VALENTINE

(denial)

I'm not. It doesn't matter to me - of course not. I was just saying...

(changing the subject)

Hey, they'll be here any minute. Let's check to be sure we know how to work these.

VAL refers to the Invisibility Cloak and Magic Digital Mirror.

PRINCE TRIPSALOT

Great idea.

VALENTINE

(tries on the invisibility cloak)

Hey, PT! Take my picture.

PRINCE TRIPSALOT

(laughing, takes a picture of the wrong part of the room)

My turn.

VALENTINE emerges. PRINCE TRIPSALOT repeats the silliness.

VALENTINE

These are so very cool!

PRINCE TRIPSALOT

(oblivious)

Mine was actually pretty warm.

Through the song, the boys hurry to hide their gear.

PRINCE TRIPSALOT

SSHH! I THINK I HEAR THEM, DON'T BE AFRAID.
WE MUSN'T FEAR THEM, FOR WE'VE GOT IT MADE.
WE'VE A DIGITAL MIRROR, AND A SPECIAL CLOAK
AND NOW WE REMEMBER WHAT THE WISE WOMAN SPOKE.

VALENTINE

OH! OH! OH! OH!
DON'T DRINK THE COCOA, WHATEVER YOU DO.

PRINCE TRIPSALOT

NO, NO, NO, NO.

VALENTINE

DON'T DRINK THE COCOA, I'M WARNING YOU.

PRINCE TRIPSALOT

NO, NO, NO, NO.

PRINCE TRIPSALOT & VALENTINE

DON'T DRINK THE COCOA, WHATEVER YOU DO.

PRINCE TRIPSALOT

NO, NO, NO, NO.

PRINCE TRIPSALOT & VALENTINE

DON'T DRINK THE COCOA, I'M WARNING YOU!

POPPY & LADY LIVIA	**TRIPSALOT & VALENTINE**
DRINK UP THE COCOA, IT'S GOOD FOR YOU.	DON'T DRINK THE COCOA, WHATEVER YOU DO.
DRINK ALL THE COCOA, WE'RE BEGGING YOU. THE COCOA IS A DELICIOUS BREW.	DON'T DRINK THE COCOA, I'M WARNING YOU. THIS COCOA IT IS A POISONED BREW!
DRINK UP THE COCOA, PLEASE DO.	... DON'T YOU!

PRINCESS POPPY & LADY LIVIA enter the boys' side of the screen with two mugs of cocoa.

PRINCESS POPPY

Good evening, good Sirs.

All ad lib pleasant greetings.

We're getting ready for sleep...

(yawns, obviously)

... and we, the Lady Livia and I, always have a cup of cocoa before bedtime. We thought you'd like some, too.

LADY LIVIA

It's very relaxing.

PRINCE TRIPSALOT

(already forgetting and reaching for his mug)

Oh, Princess, how very thoughtful of you. Oh boy! And look at all the marshmallows! I love cocoa with marshmallows!

Throughout the scene, VALENTINE keeps the PRINCE from drinking the cocoa while the PRINCE continues to try to drink it.

VALENTINE

(whisper-sings to Prince)

DON'T DRINK THE COCOA,
WHATEVER YOU DO,
DON'T DRINK THE COCOA
I'M WARNING YOU.

PRINCESS POPPY
(flirting with him to lull him into drinking the cocoa)

I love cocoa too. I have a whole lake of cocoa out in the forest.

PRINCE TRIPSALOT

I saw that. I wanted to drink some of it, but Val wouldn't let me.

PRINCESS POPPY

I put lots and lots of extra marshmallows in your cocoa tonight, just for you.

PRINCE TRIPSALOT

I LOVE marshmallows. How did you know?

PRINCESS POPPY

Just a clever guess. I love marshmallows too.

PRINCE TRIPSALOT

You do? Gee. We have so much in common.

PRINCESS POPPY
(batting eyelashes at him—she wants him to drink his cocoa)

Yeah.

VALENTINE
(notices her shoes, which are peeking out from under the robe)

Going to sleep are you, Your Princessness? You sure put on some very fancy shoes for sleeping.

PRINCESS POPPY

Oh, these old things.

(she tries to hide them under the robe)

I always wear my prettiest shoes before I go to bed.

VALENTINE
(aside to PT)

Oh sure she does.

LADY LIVIA

Won't you have some cocoa, Sir Val?

VALENTINE

Thank you, Lady Lovely... Er... I mean... Lady Livia, but we're not very thirsty.

LADY LIVIA

But Sir Val, it would make us so very happy if you tried our cocoa.

PRINCESS POPPY

Yes. It's made from the finest cocoa in the Kingdom, and the marshmallows are the blossoms of a very special marshmallow tree.

LADY LIVIA
(whisper-sings)
OH, PRINCESS, PRINCESS
I HATE TO DO IT.
OH, PRINCESS, PRINCESS
WE'RE GONNA RUE IT.

Both men hold their mugs of cocoa, as if about to drink.

VALENTINE
(aside to Prince)
Okay we've got to pretend to drink. Otherwise we'll never find out anything. But, remember, just PRETEND!

PRINCE TRIPSALOT
(aside to Valentine)
Okay. Just pretend.
(to Princess & Lady Livia)
Thank you for your kindness to us, Ladies. The cocoa smells awfully good, and look, the little marshmallows are beginning to melt. Oh, I love it when that happens.

VALENTINE
Mmm. It really does look tasty.

The men pretend to drink. A look of satisfaction passes from PRINCESS to a worried LADY LIVIA. PRINCE TRIPSALOT accidentally drinks a small amount, looks around, frantic, and VALENTINE whacks him on the back to make him spit it out, but he swallows it instead.

PRINCESS POPPY
Well, there, that's good. We'll just say goodnight, then gents.

LADY LIVIA
Goodnight.

Flirtatious looks pass between LADY LIVIA & VALENTINE. Goodnights all around.

PRINCESS POPPY & LADY LIVIA exit to the other side of the screen. PRINCESS POPPY takes off her robe, fixes her hair, readies herself to leave. LADY LIVIA does the same.

PRINCE TRIPSALOT & VALENTINE check the location of mirror & cloak, then pretend to fall asleep. The women look around the screen, see the coast is clear. They wait near the door and, by magical enchantment, the lock, the bolt and the barricade open for them. They tip-toe out.

VALENTINE gets a Mirror photo of the locks and bolts unlocking and unbolting themselves, then tries to wake PRINCE who has fallen asleep.

VALENTINE

Did you see that? Wake up PT. You didn't really drink that cocoa, did you?

PRINCE TRIPSALOT

(drowsily)

Huh? No. I… well, maybe just a sip… not much. I'm okay. Really, I am. I can make it.

VALENTINE

Okay well, hurry. They went down this passageway.

They put on their cloaks and follow the women out.

SCENE 2

A BOAT ON A MAGICAL LAKE

Entire scene is underscored.

Most of this short scene can be done with the simplest of tech – i.e., a cardboard boat cut-out with handles and room for 4 actors. It would be most effective if lit from behind a scrim. However, if no scrim is available, a boat cut-out with pin-spot on the boat and everything else in darkness will also work. For groups with larger budgets, mist can swirl around the boat as it sails across the lake, etc.

As the boat moves across the stage (the actors move it manually):

At stop 1, We see a tree with Silver Branches against the blackness (an actor in black holding the branches);

At stop 2, Golden Roses appear against the darkness (actor in black) and;

*At stop 3, Diamond Birds are seen (actor in black) and melodious bird music is heard. [**A bit of tinkly nightingale music would be nice here.]*

At each stop, the PRINCE plucks the branch, rose, bird, and hides them under his cloak, while VALENTINE snaps Mirror pictures. At first, the young men have forgotten to turn off the flash and the flash is left on. The mirror flashes once. After that no more flashes.

#11: THE MAGICAL LAKE

Instrumental Underscore.

PRINCESS sits beside LADY LIVIA who is rowing. The young men, wearing their invisible cloaks, sit directly behind each of the girls.

LADY LIVIA

The boat seems a whole lot heavier tonight than usual. What did you have for dinner?

PRINCESS POPPY

The same as you… apples and honey and roasted nut loaf. A little whole grain bread and that yummy whipped trifle for dessert.

LADY LIVIA

Well, you must've eaten a ton of it. This boat isn't moving as easily tonight as it usually does.

PRINCESS POPPY

Well don't blame me. You ate the same thing I did and you're the one who always eats too much of everything.

LADY LIVIA

That's right. Blame me. You always do.

PRINCESS POPPY

I'm a Princess. I'm allowed.

LADY LIVIA

You're also supposed to be my friend.

PRINCESS POPPY

I know. You're right. I'm sorry.

LADY LIVIA

Talk about being sorry! I hated giving Prince Tripsalot and Sir Val that drugged cocoa tonight.

PRINCESS POPPY

We had no choice. How else were we going to get away.

The boys are all ears!

LADY LIVIA

I don't know. They seemed so very nice. Maybe they would have enjoyed coming along with us and dancing with us.

PRINCESS POPPY

Livia, you know that's impossible. Only those with the Magic Kiss are allowed into the Hallowed Halls of the Divine Dance Kingdom.

LADY LIVIA

I know. I know. But, they looked so pathetic sleeping there. I just feel awful about it. It's so sad that in three short days they'll be turned into... yuk... ducks.

PRINCESS POPPY

They were foolish enough to take on the challenge, so it's no skin off my nose if they pay the price for failure. They're just dumb boys, anyway.

PT yanks at her hair.

PRINCESS POPPY

OW! Who did that?

She looks around, sees nothing, rubs her head.

Cheer up, Livia. You'll feel better about things once we get to the Ball. Look. Here we are in the Grove of Silver Trees.

At stop #1 (Silver Branches), VAL takes a photo. There is a blinding flash. The boys pantomime shutting off the flash on the mirror.

PRINCESS POPPY (CONT'D)

What was that?

LADY LIVIA

What was what?

PRINCESS POPPY

The light. I just saw a very bright flash of light.

LADY LIVIA

Oh. Well I must've missed that.

(dripping with sarcasm)

I'm too busy rowing to look around.

PRINCESS POPPY

Oh, it really startled me. I suppose it could be fireflies…

LADY LIVIA

Or shooting stars…

PRINCESS POPPY

Or the lanterns from the other boats.

LADY LIVIA

Sure. That's all it was.

At stop #1 (Silver Branches), PT grabs a branch and there is a loud snap.

PRINCESS POPPY

What was that?

LADY LIVIA

I heard that! What *was* that?

PRINCESS POPPY

I don't know! I asked you first!

LADY LIVIA

I guess… maybe… maybe… it was just the boat creaking.

PRINCESS POPPY

I guess. It's a pretty old boat. But that was a pretty loud creak. Do you think we're in danger? Do you think we're going to sink?

LADY LIVIA

No, but I'm in danger of collapsing. This boat is really heavy tonight.

PRINCESS POPPY

Well, it's not much further. Look! We've already reached the Garden of Golden Roses.

At stop #2, Golden Roses appear in the light. VALENTINE snaps a non-flash photo.

LADY LIVIA

I'm pooped. I need a rest.

PRINCESS POPPY

I hope you don't expect me to row! I am a Princess after all.

LADY LIVIA

(sarcastic)

Heavens no! The world would surely come to an end if you rowed.

(less nasty)

But maybe you could help a little?

PRINCESS POPPY

How? How can I help without getting my pretty pink hands all sore and callused?

LADY LIVIA

(sarcastic)

Oh. Right. Your hands. Well, Princess, if you want to get to the other side of the Lake, I'm going to need some help. If you've got any ideas, I'm all ears.

PRINCESS POPPY

I'll bet you forgot to do your exercises today. You know eating well alongside a healthy exercise routine is the key to strong and able bodies. I'll bet you skipped your workout.

LADY LIVIA

No. I did *not* skip anything! I worked out on my Wonderflex Machine just as I do every day. Ten reps each for my lats, tris, bis, and delts.

PRINCESS POPPY

Well, maybe it's time to *increase* your reps.

LADY LIVIA

And maybe it's time to decrease *your* intake of carbs.

PT plucks a rose. Another loud snap! He hides it under his cloak.

PRINCESS POPPY

There it is again. That loud, snapping noise. What could it be?

LADY LIVIA

How do I know? Snapping Turtles? Maybe it was my oar hitting the water harder than usual. This is the worst trip across I've ever made. My arms are so tired, Princess, I don't know if I can go any further.

PRINCESS POPPY

Well we're almost there, so don't give up.

LADY LIVIA

Maybe I'm having so much trouble because my conscience is bothering me about—well truthfully, about Val. I have to admit it, Princess, I have a bit of a crush on him.

PRINCESS POPPY

Honestly! I don't understand you. You just met him today. How can you have a crush on someone you just met?

LADY LIVIA

Didn't you ever hear of 'crush at first sight'?

PRINCESS POPPY

No, I never have.

LADY LIVIA

Tell the truth. Doesn't it bother you about all those young men who aren't good for anything anymore, at least not much more than Peking Duck?

PRINCESS POPPY

Don't be silly! Ducks don't peek. They quack. They're ducks!

LADY LIVIA

You said you liked Prince Tripsalot.

PRINCESS POPPY

It's true. I like him. He seems to have a sweet disposition. I surely like him a lot more than most of the others, but that doesn't change anything. THIS is much more important to me than any young man could be. Oh! Listen, it's the song of the Diamond Nightingales. We're almost there. I can't wait. Hurry, Livia, I can feel my feet starting to twitch.

At stop #3, Diamond Birds are seen.

VAL snaps a photo, and when PT grabs a bird to put under his cloak, the bird squawks and carries on for a brief moment before growing silent, again.

PRINCESS POPPY

Now there! That's a sound I've never heard before in all our months and months of coming here. This is too peculiar!

During this speech VAL sits beside LL, puts his arms around her and his hands on the oars, and begins to help with the rowing.

LADY LIVIA

Wow! That was a weird noise. Sounded as if one of the birds was in trouble. Oh well, it's stopped now, and you know what? Suddenly, the boat is moving more easily.

PRINCESS POPPY

Oh, good! I can hardly wait to get there.

LADY LIVIA

Look! Look! There's the shore. I can see the shore. We'll be there in no time!

PRINCESS POPPY

Finally! I can't wait!

SCENE 3

THE BALL

Entire scene is underscored with waltz music. Arrangement grows in volume and intensity as scene reaches climax.

#12: THE BALL

Instrumental Underscore.

A SCENE WITH MUSIC, DANCE AND NO DIALOGUE: In a beautiful ballroom. Elegant, stately waltz music is playing. To indicate the passage of time, as the music begins for the second time, it grows faster and faster, the dancers spin out of control and by the end, we know they've been dancing all night. If possible a very large clock should twirl from midnight to 5 AM. All the dancers end in a frenzy of collapse.

As soon as the PRINCESS arrives, she dances off with one of the young men. She switches partners frequently.

PRINCE TRIPSALOT, wearing his invisibility cloak, follows her all over the dance floor; bumping into people, tripping, falling, dancing, and most importantly, taking mirror pictures of everything. At one point, the PRINCESS begins dancing alone, and PT shadow dances with her.

LADY LIVIA stands off in a corner with the other Ladies in Waiting (i.e., the women whose partners are dancing with the PRINCESS). They dance to the music by themselves.

When the PRINCESS is shadow dancing with PT, VAL, also wearing his cloak of invisibility, shadow dances with LL.

The scene ends when all the dancers fall to the ground exhausted.

SCENE 4

THE ROYAL BEDCHAMBER,
EARLY THE NEXT MORNING

The KING is tucking into a hearty breakfast, while the QUEEN is pacing, wringing her hankie.

#13: SLEEPY PRINCESS-REPRISE

Music underscores dialogue.

KING

Hmmmph.

(mouth full of food)

These are delicious.

QUEEN

How can you eat at a time like this?

KING

What better time to eat a delicious breakfast than in the morning?

QUEEN

Don't be cute. You know what I mean!

KING

Oh, Hapless, won't you please stop pacing. You're ruining my digestion.

HE gets up and goes to soothe HER.

Why don't you just relax? Why are you fretting so?

QUEEN

Why? Why? Because this whole thing is *my fault*!

KING

Your fault? How is it your fault?

QUEEN

If I'd just *danced* with the dark wizard. Maybe if I just paid a *little* attention to him back then, maybe none of this would be happening!

KING

(soothing)

Don't be silly, my love. Be sensible. This isn't your fault. It's *HIS* fault. And, if you paid attention to him back then, there might not be an US right now and that would be just awful. Now please, come, sit down and eat something.

QUEEN

How can I sit down and eat when two more perfectly nice young valiants are about to feel an uncontrollable urge to fly south for the winter?

(singing)

ANOTHER NIGHT IS GONE, HERE WE ARE AT DAWN
WAITING FOR A HERO

KING

PRINCES COME AND GO, AND WE STILL DON'T KNOW
IF WE'RE BATTING ZERO

QUEEN

PT'S AWFULLY SWEET (WHEN HE'S ON HIS FEET)
COULD HE BE A WINNER?

KING

KEEP YOUR HOPES UP, DEAR, IT WILL ALL BE CLEAR
WHEN WE GET TO COURT

KING & QUEEN

DID SHE SLEEP, DEAR, THROUGH THE NIGHT, DEAR?
I CAN'T WAIT TO HEAR THE NEWS
WAS SHE SLEEPY, OH SO SLEEPY
OR DID SHE WEAR OUT HER SHOES?

WILL THEY BE LIKE ALL THE LOSERS
HAVING NOTHING NEW TO SAY?
WILL THEY STAY AND FACE THE MUSIC
OR WILL THEY JUST RUN AWAY?

KING

Come along my sweet. Time to find out the awful truth.

THEY start to leave.

QUEEN

(stops suddenly)

I think I should write to PT's mother and father to let them know where to pick up their ducks.

KING

Now, Hapless! Think positively. Hey, you never know. This could have a happy ending after all.

QUEEN

I do hope you're right. Let's go.

SCENE 5

THE PALACE
TWELVE NOON THE SAME DAY

PRINCESS POPPY & LADY LIVIA Enter, sleepy but cocky and sure of their victory. KING, QUEEN, CHORUS w/DUCKS all stand around dejectedly.

LADY LIVIA

I'm glad it takes three days for the transformation to occur. I don't think I could bear to see Val turned into a mallard.

PRINCESS POPPY
(yawning)

They looked so peaceful, sleeping as we left, I couldn't bring myself to disturb them.

LADY LIVIA

I hate to see them suffer.

PRINCESS POPPY

Believe it or not, me too.

LADY LIVIA

Well it took you long enough to come to your senses.

KING

Well, Daughter, where are your watchers?

PRINCESS POPPY
(yawning)

Asleep, Papa.

KING

And your shoes.

QUEEN

Just look at your shoes. Oh, Poppy. I'm so disappointed.

KING

Just like all the others. They'll slink out of here, hoping to avoid the penalty, but that won't help them. An enchantment is an enchantment after all.

QUEEN

It's really too bad. I was so hopeful.

KING

I don't know why we keep trying.

QUEEN

I don't know why *they* keep trying!

KING

It seems like such a shame to send perfectly good young men on the path to certain failure. They could be so much more useful to the Kingdom as doctors or teachers or dragonslayers.

QUEEN

Oh, well.

(resigned)

Notify the cobblers. It seems we'll be needing a gross of new shoes for the Princess after all.

KING

Send for the two young men immediately.

PRINCESS POPPY

Oh, Papa, they're still asleep… Let them sleep and enjoy their last days of happy, human dreaming.

KING

That's uncharacteristically thoughtful of you daughter. Have you had a change of heart?

PRINCESS POPPY

No, Papa. Just… well… I think that's the least reward we can give them for trying to help unravel the mystery… which, of course, they never could, but they do seem nice… and… Oh, I almost wish they might have… Oh, bother. As long as they're not going to show up, I'm going back to bed…

She turns to leave.

Enter PRINCE TRIPSALOT and VALENTINE with a great big bag of evidence, their cloaks and the Magic Digital Mirror.

CHORUS #1

(with ducks)

They're here!

CHORUS #2

But why?

CHORUS #3

You'd think they'd slink off home before the transformation.

CHORUS #4

Look! What are they dragging?

CHORUS #5

Shh. Let's listen and hear what's going on.

PRINCE TRIPSALOT

Good Morning, Majesties, Princess, Lady Livia, Members of the Court…

ALL

(stunned but wary)

Good Morning.

KING

You're still here!

PRINCE TRIPSALOT

Of course, your Royalness.

QUEEN

I'm impressed. None of the others ever came to Court on the morning after they tried to find out how the Princess's shoes became so tattered.

PRINCE TRIPSALOT

I guess that was because they didn't have the answer.

KING

WHAT!?

Startled commotion.

QUEEN

Are you saying you KNOW what happens to her shoes?

PRINCE TRIPSALOT

I am. Yes. That's exactly what I'm saying. I know what happens to her shoes.

Commotion—ad libbed amazement and surprise, doubt, etc.

PRINCESS POPPY

Impossible. You can't know anything. We left you sleeping soundly when we...

(she catches herself and stops)

I don't believe it. You can't know. You're making up a story just so my father will give you half his Kingdom.

PRINCE TRIPSALOT

Princess, just so I will be believed and not thought ill of by you, I do hereby relinquish my claim and all entitlement to any part of your father's wealth or his Kingdom. That wasn't the reason I volunteered for this. I did this for the Greater Good. I did it for the adventure. I did it because of *Noblesse Oblige*. I did it because it's really boring in my Kingdom. But mostly, I did it because I wanted to get to know you better.

PRINCESS POPPY

(softening)

You mean you really don't want my father's wealth?

PRINCE TRIPSALOT

Not a Ducat.

PRINCESS POPPY

Or his Kingdom?

PRINCE TRIPSALOT

Not a duck.

KING

Very nice. Very nice. But we still haven't had a single answer to the mystery.

PRINCESS POPPY

That's true. Maybe you're just saying all this in the hope that we'll rip up the contract and you won't be transformed. Well, it's too late for that. You signed. You're committed. Nice guy or not, in three days time you'll be a drake.

PRINCE TRIPSALOT

Then, if you'll allow me... everyone, get comfortable, this is a kind of long story. Val.

VALENTINE joins him and they begin their story, using appropriate proofs as the story unfolds. An overhead screen and slide projector or PowerPoint presentation should be used to project some of the things the Magic Digital Mirror saw, large enough for the audience to see.

#14: THE MYSTERY SOLVED

Song is done "Film Noir" style, with VALENTINE doing a "Bogart" accent to LADY LIVIA.

VALENTINE

(spoken, with underscoring)

You see, Schweetheart, we heard about this mystery back home, see. And so started for your kingdom some days ago!

PRINCE TRIPSALOT

ALONG THE WAY WE DID MEET
A TERRIBLE WRETCHED BEAST
WITH ITS LEG IN A SNARE.

Slide #1: Picture of TWB ensnared.

BRAVE AND NOBLE AS I AM I SET THE POOR CREATURE FREE.

VALENTINE

Ahem.

PRINCE TRIPSALOT

I MEAN MY VALET AND ME.

Slide #2: PRINCE TRIPSALOT, VALENTINE & TWB with arms around one another—a buddy photo. TWB is in the bear suit.

IT TURNED OUT THAT THE BEAST WASN'T A MONSTER AT ALL
BUT THE WISE JELLAHNDRA, ENCHANTRESS FAIR,

Slide #3: PRINCE TRIPSALOT, VALENTINE & JELLAHNDRA, out of the bear suit.

WHO'D BEEN IMPRISONED BY THAT DARK WIZARD OF YOURS...

VALENTINE

... THE VERY SAME WHO ENCHANTED YOU.

PRINCE TRIPSALOT

ONCE WE RELEASED HER FROM HER TRAP,
SHE TOLD US ALL ABOUT THE MYSTERY OF POPPY'S SHOES...

VALENTINE

... Well, not quite everything.

PRINCE TRIPSALOT

That's right. That would be cheating. And I *never* cheat!

KING

Well, get on with it!

QUEEN

What was it? How did you find out? What happens to her shoes?

PRINCE TRIPSALOT

JELLAHNDRA GAVE US ADVICE,
BUT FIRST SHE GAVE THIS DEVICE . . .

He holds up the Mirror.

VALENTINE

... WITH CLOAKS THAT MAKE US UNSEEN.

Slide #4: Jellahndra with her arms around two empty spaces.

VALENTINE holds up the Cloaks of Invisibility and the Digital Magic Mirror—but the crowd doesn't get it—so he slips it on, and 'disappears.' Everyone ooohs and aaahhhs. He removes the cloak.

CHORUS

Ooh! Aah!

PRINCE TRIPSALOT

WITH THESE WE FOLLOWED THE GIRLS...

VALENTINE

BUT NOT BEFORE WE'D PRETEND
TO DRINK THE COCOA THEY GAVE.

PRINCE TRIPSALOT

That's right! It was drugged with a sleeping potion!

Slide #5: Girls drugging cocoa.

KING

HEY! BUT I BOLTED AND I LOCKED AND I BARRICADED
THE DOORS MYSELF. HOW DID YOU GET FREE?

PRINCE TRIPSALOT

THE LOCKS AND BOLTS AND BARRICADE,
THEY WERE MAGIC'D TOO,
ENCHANTED BY THE DARK WIZARD'S HAND.

VALENTINE

THE PRINCE AND I FOLLOWED THE GIRLS TO A WAITING BOAT
AND ROWED ACROSS THE ENCHANTED LAKE.

Slide #6: The boat on the lake with the ladies getting into it.

LADY LIVIA

I told you that boat was heavier than usual! "Too much trifle!" Hmm!

PRINCE TRIPSALOT

FIRST WE PASSED INTO A GROVE, A GROVE OF SILVER TREES.
THIS WAS THE FIRST THING WE DID SEE.

PRINCESS POPPY

This is a lovely Fairy Tale, but you have no proof!

PRINCE TRIPSALOT

Yes. We do.

He shows the mirror pictures, including the flash.

Slide # 7: PT hands the KING a Silver Branch. VV projects a Digital Magic photo from the Mirror. Everyone ooohs and aaahhhs.

PRINCESS POPPY

OH, NO! OH, NO! THE FLASH!

LADY LIVIA

OH, YES! OH, YES! THE FLASH!

PT shows the Golden Roses.

Slide # 8: PRINCE hands the PRINCESS a Golden Rose, then VALENTINE projects a Digital Magic photo from the Mirror. Everyone ooohs and aaahhhs.

PRINCE TRIPSALOT

AFTER THE SILVER TREES WE SAILED ON TO THESE.
GOLDEN ROSES, A GARDEN FILLED WITH THESE.

PRINCESS POPPY

That's what those snapping noises were!

LADY LIVIA

At least it wasn't the boat cracking!

PRINCE TRIPSALOT

THEN WE SAILED ALONG UNTIL WE HEARD A SONG
THE DIAMOND NIGHTINGALE, A LOVELY MELODY.

Slide #9: PT hands a Diamond Nightingale to the Queen and it begins to sing its lovely melody. VV projects a photo from the Digital Mirror. More ooohs and aaahs.

PRINCE TRIPSALOT (CONT'D)

WE FINALLY CAME TO THE SHORE,
BUT KNEW NOT WHAT LAY IN STORE
SO WE REMAINED OUT OF VIEW.
AN ESCORT THEN LED THE WAY
WHERE ALL THE DANCERS DID SWAY
FOR THERE THE MUSIC DID PLAY.

VALENTINE projects an assortment of photos from the dance, many of them close-ups of LADY LIVIA, but enough of the PRINCESS and her assorted partners to convince the KING and QUEEN.*

**Any number of slides can be used to show the dance.*

THEY WERE ESCORTED TO A BALLROOM OF SPLENDID SIZE
WITH WHIRLING AND TWIRLING...

VALENTINE

... IT DIZZIED THE EYES

PRINCE TRIPSALOT

WHERE POPPY DANCED EVERY DANCE WITH A DIFFERENT GUY
ALL THROUGH THE NIGHT...

VALENTINE

... BOY, THEY SWARMED LIKE FLIES!

PRINCE TRIPSALOT

THE SWIRLING DANCE GREW, AND IT GREW,
WE WERE SWALLOWED WHOLE
WHILE POPPY KEPT ON WEARING OUT HER SOLES.

PRINCE TRIPSALOT & VALENTINE

NOW WITH OUR MAGICAL DIGITAL MIRROR,
WE'RE TELLING YOU.

PRINCE TRIPSALOT

And that, your Royal King and Queenness, is the reason for the terrible condition of your daughter's shoes, and also the reason she's so tired every day. Thus solves the Mystery of Princess Poppy's Shoes!

Everyone but KING, QUEEN, & PRINCESS applaud.

KING

Is this true, Daughter?

PRINCESS POPPY

Yes, Papa. I cannot tell a lie. Prince Tripsalot has discovered the truth and revealed my secret.

LADY LIVIA

Does this mean the spell is broken?

PRINCESS POPPY

I hope so. We'll know better when I go check the golden ponies. But Papa, I must admit, I'll miss the Ball and all the handsome partners. Staying up all night. Sigh. It was so thrilling. But, you know, I'd sure like to have a little time to go out in the daylight and read and play and take long walks in the warm sunshine.

LADY LIVIA

Imagine, a daytime walk in the park!

PRINCESS POPPY & LADY LIVIA

And a good night's sleep for a change!

KING

Then, Prince Tripsalot, er... PT, You have solved the mystery and we are forever in your debt. If you won't take half my gold or half my Kingdom, how can we ever repay you?

PRINCE TRIPSALOT

Well, Sire, now that I'm not going to be splashing around in orange sauce, as I said when I first arrived, I'd like to be able to hang around and get to know Princess Poppy a little better.

KING

Well, Poppy, what about it?

PRINCESS POPPY

(shyly)

I don't see why not.

(to PT)

Do you like to dance?

#15: THERE'S A WORLD OUT THERE-REPRISE

ALL

COME ON, THERE'S A WORLD OUT THERE,
TIME TO RISE AND PLAY
YOU ONLY GET ONE CHANCE MY FRIEND,
DON'T LET IT SLIP AWAY.
COME ON AND FEEL THE SUN UPON YOUR FACE.
DON'T YOU TELL ME THAT YOU HATE TO WAKE!
AMAZING ADVENTURES WILL AWAIT YOU THERE!

FROM GOLD SWINGS THAT GRANT WISHES,
FLYING FISH THAT CROON TUNES
TO THE TREES GROWING BON BONS IN A
CHOCOLATE LAGOON,
YOU'LL MISS ALL OF THE WONDERS LYING
THERE IN YOUR BED,
HIDING UNDER YOUR COCOON!

BLACKOUT.

Lights up for Curtain Call.

ALL

AMAZING ADVENTURES STILL AWAIT YOU THERE!
STILL AWAIT YOU THERE! STILL AWAIT YOU THERE!

END OF PLAY

Additional titles from Steele Spring Stage Rights

Book & Lyrics by ALISON McGARRY | Music by BRIAN LEADER

Family Musical | 4F, 2M, Ensemble | 75 minutes

"Delightfully humorous, clever, and catchy!" –*On Stage*

In this new twist on the old pony-tale, Rapunzel is more than just a damsel in distress who's long overdue for a haircut; she's a daring and precocious little lass who is determined to solve her own problems. A garden of magical singing fruits and vegetables, a wisecracking rat, a good-hearted bluebird, a sage cricket, a vast variety of bugs, and a fidgety flying squirrel (who can't fly) all help her along the way to "everything turning out right." Young thespians and adults alike will fall in love with the wacky, entertaining characters in this imaginative new fairytale musical.

Book by TONY JERRIS | Music & Lyrics by CORINNE AQUILINA

Family Musical | 1F, 6 M or F, Ensemble | 60 minutes

"A big success! Clever, tuneful and entertaining!" –*Gannett Newspaper*

The Easter Bunny better hop quickly, Santa Claus better hold on to his trousers, and the whole barnyard better sing the blues because one little witch can't get her fill of tricks. This mischievous little wonder wishes every day was Halloween and creates witching mayhem wherever she goes. All seems to be going her way until a giant spider and a rapping record producer step into the picture, and The Littlest Witch must learn to play nice to see who her real friends are. With a whimsical score and clever book, *The Littlest Witch* rises to every holiday occasion. **"Funny and innocent enough for children, but enough adult humor for the whole family!"** –*Brighton-Pittsford Post*

www.stagerights.com

Additional titles from Steele Spring Stage Rights

Book, Music & Lyrics by PETER SHAM | Music by RANDALL KRAMER
Additional Script Material by STEVEN D'ADDIECO

Family Musical | 5F, 9M, Ensemble | 90 minutes

"A howling entertainment success!" –*The Buffalo Evening News*

With a street quality like a modern-day *Oliver!,* this charming musical follows the adventures of a golden retriever named Bo as he works his way out of a sticky situation. Bo meets cuddly friends and growling enemies along his journey to a heartwarming and happy ending. *It's a Dog's Life* is "doggone" fun for the whole family with great music that will have your audience humming as they walk up the aisle. **"Inspired and entertaining!"** –*Buffalo Courier Express*

By ADAM NEUBAUER and SAMANTHA LEVENSHUS

Family Comedy | 5F, 6M, Ensemble | 75 minutes

"A demented mash-up of the Brothers Grimm!" –*Backstage*

Enter the familiar world of "Once Upon a Time," as a chipper Minstrel takes you (and a small, curious boy) on a journey of epic proportions. In a magical forest we find the characters from the Grimm's tales; Hansel & Gretel, Snow White, Cinderella, and The Frog Prince all working their way toward their own happy endings. Along the journey, their tales collide at a breakneck pace, keeping these age-old stories feeling fresh for the 21st century. Devilishly funny and brimming with wit, *The Grimm World* is family-friendly entertainment that promises to bring out the kid in everyone. **"Colorful and entertaining, with a large heaping of humor."** –*Life in LA*

www.stagerights.com

Additional titles from Steele Spring Stage Rights

Adapted for the stage by MARK LANDON SMITH | 5F, 9M, Ensemble | 70 minutes

A side-splitting adaptation of the classic cult film!

This is it! The stage adaptation of Ed Wood's *Plan 9 From Outer Space*, considered by many to be "the worst movie ever made!" Packing B-Movie thrills into 70 action-packed minutes, the story goes something like this: visiting space soldiers use a magic-electro-space-ray-gun to resurrect a recently deceased (and perfectly ghoulish) human couple, putting "Plan 9" into action. The aliens must stop mankind from developing "Solaramite," a substance that could set off a chain reaction of cosmic explosions that would destroy the entire universe. With "Plan 9" activated, the space aliens step up the action: Flying saucers invade! Hollywood reacts! The Pentagon responds! Even Colonel Sanders tries to stop the aliens and, well, this was absolutely the worst movie ever made. You'll have a blast with this cosmic comedy perfect for all producing groups.

Created by WILLIAM A. REILLY and GARY LAMB

Family Musical | 4F, 5M | 2 hours, 5 minutes

"Fun, fun, fun!! Truly great entertainment." *–Broadwayworld.com*

An exciting musical romp based on *Charley's Aunt,* featuring nostalgic favorites such as "Daisy Bell (A Bicycle Built for Two)," "Aba Daba Honeymoon," "You Made Me Love You," and, of course, the title tune, "I'm Just Wild About Harry." In turn-of-the-century Milwaukee, Jack and Harry need a chaperone so they can entertain their sweethearts. Enter their friend Benjamin to impersonate Harry's Aunt, a rich widow from Brazil. Hilarity ensues when Harry's Aunt actually arrives on the scene, and this musical farce of mistaken identity and madcap adventure climaxes in a delightfully happy conclusion.

www.stagerights.com

Additional titles from Steele Spring Stage Rights

Book & Lyrics by BERT BERNARDI | Music by JUSTIN RUGG

Family Musical | 5F, 3M, Ensemble | 70 minutes

This purrrfect crime-fighting musical is the cat's meow!

Mild-mannered kitties by day; crime-stopping cats by night! This family-friendly pop musical spoofs the likes of television serials from *Charlie's Angels* to *Batman*! Set in a campy make-believe world, each act features a different adventure for our glamorous trio of crime-fighters: act one finds our colorful kitties seeking out a treasured trinket that's mysteriously missing; act two lands our fetching felines in a side-splitting canary caper, complete with flying feathers. This new musical is truly a laugh-a-minute adventure for audiences of all ages.

The Brothers Grimm and a SHOWGIRL

Book & Lyrics by BERT BERNARDI | Music by JUSTIN RUGG

Family Musical | 1F, 3M | 70 minutes

An enchanting and quick-witted twist on the classics!

This wildly imaginative new family musical features spoofs and goofs of all your favorite fairy tales! Meet Jacob, Wilhelm and George—The Brothers Grimm themselves!—all set to present their best-known stories. But when they forget their book of fairy tales, the fun really starts. Add a sequined and feathered Showgirl to help the guys, and you've got a great big comedy hit! Featuring exciting versions of "Little Red Riding Hood," "Snow White," "Rapunzel" and "Sleeping Beauty," the fun leads to a delightfully nonsensical and audience-inspired story called "Das Rumpleshperlinschpee." Fast-paced and inventive, this is the most 'happy ever after' show around!

www.stagerights.com

Additional titles from Steele Spring Stage Rights

Book & Lyrics by BERT BERNARDI | Music by JUSTIN RUGG

Family Musical | 3F, 4M | 75 minutes

"Kids love pirates—and so will you!" –*Connecticut Post*

Ahoy, Mateys! Get ready for a wildly comical ride as three lovely ladies are cursed by a soggy old sea hag to live as pirates on a tropical isle. When their tiny ship, the Michele Lee, arrives on the island, the beauties discover three handsome princes who have fallen under a similar curse! All six are in search of a magical unicorn who can provide them with a potion that could set everything right again. Their antics, foibles, and foolery provide for a host of swashbuckling songs and situations, blunders, plunders, and happy endings. The story spills from the stage into the aisles, allowing for clever interactions with the audience in the true spirit of the panto. Yo ho!

Book and Lyrics by ROB. LAUER | Music by MATT BEAN

Family Musical | 2F, 6M | 65 minutes

A zany musical comedy for the entire family!

Hans Christian Anderson's tale of an Emperor who's a slave to fashion is expanded and turned on its head! Lampooning everything from high fashion and pretentious celebrities, to pompous politicians and con artists, this whimsical show has delighted hundreds of thousands of kids, teens, and adults across the country. With music evocative of the Golden Age of Broadway mixed with modern comic sensibilities, this delightfully madcap musical comedy will have kids (and adults) of all ages roaring with laughter!

www.stagerights.com

Additional titles from Steele Spring Stage Rights

Book & Lyrics by BERT BERNARDI | Music by JUSTIN RUGG

Holiday Family Musical | 5F, 4M, 11 Girls | 80 minutes

The Little Miss Christmas Pageant Musical

This fresh and funny new musical offers an inside peek at the mother-daughter hijinks behind the fiercely competitive "Little Miss Christmas Pageant," where ten girls (and their outrageous mothers) compete for the crown. Take a bevy of beauty winner wannabes in ruffled socks and black patent leather shoes, mix in sequins, ambition, and some pushy, frantic mothers, and you have all the ingredients for a ridiculously entertaining musical comedy! In the end, your audiences will feel the Christmas spirit as the mothers and daughters learn the value of truth and honesty in this heartwarming new holiday classic.

Book by MARK CABANISS | Music and Lyrics by LOWELL ALEXANDER

Based on the screenplay "It's a Wonderful Life"
by Frances Goodrich, Albert Hackett and Frank Capra

Holiday Family Musical | 2F, 5M, Ensemble | 2 hours

"A heartwarming, musical holiday treat!" *–The Asheville Citizen-Times*

The beloved American film, *It's a Wonderful Life,* is transformed into a joyful and stirring new holiday classic! George Bailey dreams of travel and adventure, but circumstances keep him trapped in his hometown. Frustrated by life and haunted by an impending scandal, George prepares to end his life on Christmas Eve, but a heavenly messenger arrives to show him a vision: what the world would have been like if he had never been born. If it's true that every time a bell rings, an angel has earned its wings, then this winning and heavenly musical rings its own bells and flies high above the crowd. **"This show is some kind of wonderful!"** *–Bold Life Magazine*

www.stagerights.com

Additional titles from Steele Spring Stage Rights

Book & Lyrics by BERT BERNARDI | Music by JUSTIN RUGG

Holiday Family Musical | 4F, 4M | 80 minutes

"Entertaining for all ages!" – Connecticut Post

Teen Santa is a fast-paced and wildly inventive new holiday musical, chronicling the life of seventeen-year-old Chris, who discovers that his super-hero powers of faith, hope and charity often turn him into a teenage Santa Claus! Set in Chris' garage with a live onstage band, the show cleverly uses props and clutter from the garage to create the present, the past, and several comic book-style fantasy sequences. This is the perfect holiday show for a highly creative production team, and your teen cast members will love the theatrical, punk rock-flavored score. *Teen Santa* is a uniquely entertaining musical that will prove to one and all that belief in the spirit of Christmas can change the world!

By ROGER BEAN | Musical | 4F | 52 minutes

Make it home by curfew in this one act version of the off-Broadway hit!

Wonderettes '58 takes you to the 1958 Springfield High School prom where we meet the Wonderettes, four girls with hopes and dreams as big as their crinoline skirts! As we learn about their lives and loves, we are treated to the girls performing such classic '50s songs as "Lollipop," "Dream Lover," "Stupid Cupid," "Lipstick On Your Collar," "Hold Me, Thrill Me, Kiss Me," and other classic hits! You've never had this much fun at a prom and you will never forget *Wonderettes '58*—a must-take musical trip down memory lane! This delightful 55-minute version of the smash off-Broadway hit is perfect for both teens and adults. **"It doesn't get any better than this!"** –*WOR Radio*

www.stagerights.com

16555553R00041

Made in the USA
Middletown, DE
17 December 2014